Girl,
GET IT
TOGETHER

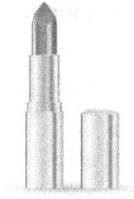

AMBER DEE

GIRL, GET IT TOGETHER
Copyright © 2016 by Amber Dee/Passion and Purpose Publishing

Edited by Val Pugh
Cover Design by Ana Grigoriu
Interior Design by Anita Jovanović

Printed in the United States of America
First Printing, 2016
ISBN (paperbook): 978-0-9973236-0-3
ISBN (e-book): 978-0-9973236-1-0
Passion and Purpose Publishing

If you would like to use material from the book (other than for review purposes), please direct your inquiries to: passionandpurposepublishing@gmail.com

Printed in the United States

To my husband, **Brandon**.
Thank you for standing by me.

To my mother, **Chearl**.
Your love for me is unconditional.
Thank you for believing in me.

CONTENTS

"If you are not willing **TO RISK** the unusual, you will have to settle for the ordinary."

-JIM ROHN

To the girls that want to make a change in their lives by going after what they want, I want to congratulate you. You may not hear it but you are awesome. From the top of your head to the bottom of your feet, you are beautifully unique and nothing or no one can stop you from reaching your dreams. You have everything you need within you. I hope in these pages you find your light to your path and your wings to soar. Thank you for letting me be a part of your journey.

-Amber

INTRODUCTION

"The best thing a girl can have is her shit together."

-AUTHOR UNKNOWN

HEY GIRL! Yes, I'm talking to you. You see, I feel comfortable greeting you like I've known you forever, because I have. I know all about your thoughts, your feelings, your beliefs, and even your secret fears without ever meeting you. How, you ask? Because I have been *you* for quite some time now. Don't believe me? Here, I'll prove it. Tell me if this sounds familiar:

* You feel as if you are stuck in neutral, not getting to the life you want.

* You marvel at the thought of living a laptop lifestyle.

9

* You are a seeker of a new way of thinking, living, and being.

* You have found yourself just going through the motions.

* You know you have a purpose higher than going to work just to pay bills.

* You want to enjoy all that life has to offer without having to plan years in advance.

* You have told yourself the following over and over again:

  * *"I'm over this."*
  * *"I need a change."*
  * *"I need to get it together."*

Told ya! I know all about you. We're practically twins. Let's call ourselves the dynamic duo. Oh wait! Better yet, let's call ourselves the determined-dignified-destined-for-greatness duo. What?! Is that too much? Okay... Okay... I'll scale it back. Let's just say we are alike in many ways, and this time the feat of getting it together is going to be different. Seriously! This is one ride that you will stay on until the end. You've thought to yourself: *Enough is enough! It's time for me to get it together.* Well, that's just what this guide will help us do.

While reading this, you will take back your life and get on the right path to your passion-filled, purposeful destination. Okay, so I know there isn't a shortage of material on the market about goal setting. However, this book is not your ordinary goal-setting book. You won't read extreme terms about scientific reasoning for how the brain works, nor will you read the formula that will make you "get it together" overnight. Nope! You're not going to read that here. What you will read here is *real* girl talk about our downfalls, our challenges, our strengths, and our uniqueness of being women. We'll also learn ways to use them to our advantage to create the extraordinary lives we want.

Girl, I know it's difficult trying to balance everything you have going on in your life #thestruggleisreal. Juggling life and the multiple factors that come with being a woman can be exhausting. Some days, you just don't feel like getting out of your pajamas or leaving your house, much less adding more stuff to your plate that runneth over. Trust me - I *get* it. And, let's not mention the "I'll start next week" mindset. I mean, we attempt to plan our lives and hope that everything will work out. However, that's like tossing a penny into a well and praying that our lives will magically change overnight. *Thinking* does not equal *doing*, and we're not making a movie or living in utopia. This is real life.

I recently heard someone ask, "If there are five frogs on a log and one decides to jump off, how many frogs are on the log?" This one seems pretty easy and obvious that if one jumps off, then there are four frogs left; however, here's the thing. Making a decision is not an action; therefore, there are five frogs still on that log. You have to do more than just *decide* that you want to change. You have to make the steps and take action. The process will take some time, but the results are worth it. Beyoncé wasn't built overnight, so why would you think you could do it quick and easy?! I know it's overwhelming and slightly daunting to think about the challenges you'll face, but this transformation won't be quick nor will it be easy. If anyone tells you the opposite, THEY'RE LYING! It will take determination, dedication, and persistence to get you there. The good thing is that you already have everything inside of you that you need to be successful.

Now, when I refer to success, it's not just the success of money. It's the success of you reaching your goals and creating more for yourself. Are you ready to leave that 9 to 5 rat race? Do you have a goal to lose weight? How about a goal to be a straight "A" student? Maybe you have a goal to take your career to another level or even to change your career. Whatever your goal is, you define your success. You are in control of your victory with each goal you set. *Side note: This notion should have you beaming right now… isn't "control" our favorite word?! #GIRLPOWER*

Okay, I think we're on the same page about our struggles, so let's not delay this thing any longer – let's move to getting *ish* done. If you are anything like me, which clearly has already been determined, you're probably thinking: *Well, Amber… I know what I'm doing wrong, but how do I fix it? How can I be successful?* I'm with you on that thought. No one ever told me *how* to set and reach a goal. No one said there is a particular way. I was constantly asking what goals I should set, and how to know if the goals I set were right for me. Most importantly, I asked how can I succeed with my goals.

This book will get your brain gears rolling into the mental shift that is needed to create, conduct, and complete a goal. You will become a girl that has her life together. Any goal you set from here forth will be a piece of cake. By learning the fundamentals and building blocks of setting and achieving goals, you will put yourself a step ahead in the game. You *will* accomplish anything that your heart desires, as long as you're willing to work for it. Now, are you ready to morph into the "it" girl that has it together? Of course you are, so with no further delay, let's get it together!

1

MAKE A DECISION

*"IT'S **YOUR PLACE** IN THE WORLD;
IT'S **YOUR LIFE.** GO ON AND DO **ALL YOU CAN**
WITH IT, AND MAKE IT THE LIFE YOU **WANT** TO LIVE."*
—Mae Jemison

I CAN'T BEGIN to tell you the countless times I have set a goal to lose weight, to wake up early, to stop eating meat, to start my own business, etc....the list goes from California to Georgia and back again. I always thought I really wanted those things; however, looking back, I only wanted them in my mind. I wasn't prepared to give up or to take on the things that came with those goals. If I saw a slice of pizza, I would eat it and think: *Well, it's just one slice.* If I needed to take extra time to attend an entrepreneur workshop during the week, I would think: *I'm too tired. I'll go next time.* If I woke up at 6:00 a.m., I would tell myself, "*Ten more minutes.*" I'm sure you know those ten minutes turned into an hour and half. That one slice of pizza turned into two (or three...yikes!)

and I never got around to attending the workshop the next time around. My behavior was not matching what I *said* or *thought* I wanted. I mean, yes, those things would be excellent in real life, but let's be honest - I wasn't ready.

> *You can't have a million-dollar dream with a minimum-wage work ethic.*
>
> -Stephen Hogan

I was unaware of what it truly took to successfully accomplish those goals I had set for myself. It's been said that it takes twenty-one days to form a habit, and I couldn't get pass day two. It had become obvious that I was on a train, quickly headed to nowhere station. The motivation, effort, and sacrifice that I needed to succeed were not there. Like so many of us, I made empty promises to myself, only to have them end in defeat. I would constantly beat myself up about it. I didn't understand what was going on but after so many attempts ending in failure, I learned to adjust and move on with my life.

On PsychologyToday.com, Carl Beuke, Ph.D. discussed the difference between a high achiever and a less accomplished individual. He stated that high achievers "have a strong desire to accomplish something important and gain gratification from success." According to Dr. Beuke, high achievers say things such as, "Don't assume that you can't do something until you've tried. I mean really tried - like tried 3000 times; not that you tried three times, and said, 'Oh, I give up.' " Unlike high achievers, Dr. Beuke stated, "Less accomplished individuals are less likely to attempt achievement-oriented tasks, and may give up quickly if success is not readily forthcoming. Less accomplished individuals tend to think that a task is not possible. Therefore, they procrastinate, give less than their best effort, or engage in other self-handicapping behaviors that provide a face-saving excuse in the event of failure."

Fact

Procrastination is not only associated with negative consequences for the activity being delayed but is also related to decreased well-being, poorer mental health, lower performance, and financial difficulties.

I think it is safe to say that desire is necessary if you truly want to be successful with accomplishing your goals. In addition, the goals you set should be none other than your own. Throughout your life, I'm sure someone probably has given you unsolicited advice about what you *should* do with your life. I was a victim of the *should* committee, and I despised it. You *should* go to college. You *should* work a 9 to 5. You *should* be married. You *should* have children.

My younger self would completely submit to what others thought I *should* do. I would change my hair if someone thought it wasn't a good fit. I would change my clothes if someone thought my outfit wasn't popping. Through all of that, I lost myself and my identity. I had to learn to block out the opinions of others and live life for myself. I eventually began to accept myself, and I embraced the motto that **"the opinion of others is not my reality."**

Tip

Say **NO** to *things* and *people* that are not in line with your vision.

I recently read about Annie Lawless, the twenty-seven year old co-founder of Suja Life. This cold juice pressing company was recently invested in via a very lucrative deal. Annie and her co-founders made millions and the company is currently valued at $300 million. That's a nice chuck of moolah! Think about being a millionaire while you are still in your twenties. That's phenomenal, but this success almost never made it to fruition.

Before becoming a millionaire, Annie struggled with getting out of bed, and she was completely tired of her life as a law student. Though she excelled in her class, deep down, she didn't have a desire to be a lawyer. As a child, she was diagnosis with celiac disease that caused her to lacked nutrients and energy. She decided to study nutrition and researched different methods to gain additional nutrients in her life. This is where the idea of the cold juice press was born.

Because of her desire, Annie pursued an education in health and became a certified holistic health coach. Still, in spite of her obvious passion, she went to law school to chase a dream that would make her family proud. In an interview, she stated that she was worried that if she followed an unconventional path, her family wouldn't understand it and would think less of her or be disappointed in her choice. Luckily, she wised up and realized that her life's desire was based on what she wanted, not what someone else wanted for her life.

Like Annie, many of us get confused about what type of goals to set. We may be influenced by our parents or feel pressure to live a particular lifestyle based on what we see on television or social media. If you are setting a goal because of what someone told you or something you see, then your path will be a rocky one and quite possibly an unsuccessful one as well. Completing goals take a lot of hard work and dedication. You *must* have a desire and be starving for the taste of success; if not, you're wasting time. The goals you set should come from deep within, so get clear on why you are doing this.

ACTION:

GET CLARITY ON
WHAT YOU *want*

1. Write a list of **20** things you *want* to accomplish in life - **20** things you *love* to do or **20** things you want to *have.*

2. Now, go back and prioritize the list from most to least important.

3. Place a star beside the *top* (5) items.

4. From that top (5) list, choose one goal that you have *the most desire* to accomplish – i.e. willing to do whatever it takes to achieve this goal.

"I HAVE THE POWER TO MAKE CHANGES IN MY LIFE"

2

WHAT'S MY MOTIVATION

*"WE ARE WHAT WE REPEATEDLY DO. **EXCELLENCE, THEN, IS NOT AN ACT, BUT A HABIT.**"*

—*Aristotle*

NOW THAT YOU KNOW what you want to accomplish, and you are excited about getting there, what's going to keep that excitement burning? What's going to keep you going even when you feel like giving up? Let's be honest, the desire to quit will come, so you need to determine your motivation.

Motivation is literally the desire to do things. It's the difference between waking up before dawn to pound the pavement and lazing around the house all day. It's the crucial element in setting and attaining goals; and, to be successful with any goals, you have to have the desire to achieve the goals you have set.

As humans, we tend to find a routine and stick to it. When we find something that works, it's hard for us to change it. If you have trained yourself to wake up every morning at 7:00 AM to get your day started, you may find it difficult to change your start time to 5:00 AM. If you are accustomed to having dessert after dinner, it may a little difficult to stop eating it all together. Our brains look for routines to create a habit that will become an automatic impulse. We lack what is needed to take us to the next level, because of the inability to control our impulses. We continue to repeat that same pattern of behavior that we absolutely hate, because we reinforce that behavior by continuously repeating it.

Driving home is a great example of how our brains automate our behaviors. You probably don't notice the way you are actually driving, because your brain has programmed your route, and it is now routine. It's your brain's way of putting your behaviors on autopilot. You don't have to think about it. The behavioral patterns we have repeated are now etched into our neural pathways. This is identical to how habits are formed. I'm sure you've heard that old habits, good or bad, are hard to break and new habits are hard to form.

Fact

Your brain tries to find things that you do all the time and learn to do them automatically to free your thoughts for something else.

Since our brains love routine, we have to retrain our brains for success. Retraining your brain is not rocket science and numerous amounts of people have done it before you. Their desire kept them going. When setting your goals, it's necessary to know *why* you want to reach this goal - and not just because it sounds good. You have to have passion for this success, because inevitably, you're going to need it. The desire that you have to reach that goal will drive your self-discipline. Take the following self-discipline test to see if you need improvement.

SELF-DISCIPLINE TEST

Rate yourself on the scale by selecting one of the following: **DS** – *disagree strongly*, **D** – *disagree*, **N** – *neutral*, **A** – *agree*, or **AS** – *agree strongly*.

	DS	D	N	A	AS
1. I have a strong sense of purpose	1	2	3	4	5
2. Life's a drag when you are always chasing goals.	5	4	3	2	1
3. My long-range plans in life are well-established.	1	2	3	4	5
4. It is difficult for me to picture an event in my mind before it occurs.	5	4	3	2	1
5. When success is near, I can almost taste, feel, and see it.	1	2	3	4	5
6. I consult my daily planner almost every day.	1	2	3	4	5

7. My days rarely turn out the way I planned.
5 4 3 2 1

8. What I do for a living isn't nearly as important as the money it pays.
5 4 3 2 1

9. Some parts of my job are as exciting to me as a hobby.
1 2 3 4 5

10. I feel energized when I have a new goal to pursue.
1 2 3 4 5

Calculate your score by adding up the numbers you have selected that best describes you.

40-50 points – You are highly self-disciplined person.

30-39 points – You have an average degree of self-discipline.

20-29 points – You may be experiencing some difficulty with self-discipline.

1-19 points – You have enough problems with self-discipline to limit achieving many of the things in life that are important to you.

NOTE: *This is a condensed version of the original test. Scores may vary in accuracy.*

After taking the test, what do your scores reveal about you? Do you need more self-discipline to ensure you are successful with reaching your goal, or are you right on track? Do whatever you must to get your heels clacking on your destination path. You're going to need momentum to finish this race. Another way that has worked for many with continued motivation is by constantly reminding yourself of the bigger picture. Knowing the reason you started in the first place is a great way to keep your heels on the pedal.

> *Let the fact that you're not where you want to be, motivate your hustle.*

The reasons you list for reaching your goal should elicit a yearning to be consistent in your journey. Your chances of staying connected and motivated to reach these goals are much higher when you frequently review this list. Are you trying to increase your income to provide a better life for yourself or your family? Are you creating a goal that will increase your health? Maybe your goal is to repair a relationship. Whatever it is, use it for visualization. Better yet, create a vision board for your goals. Put up a happy picture of you and the other person if you're working on repairing a relationship. Maybe your goal is to get back to the size you were five years ago. Put up a picture of yourself during that time, and view it every day. These are steps to help you visualize the feeling of achieving your goals. These steps go along great when creating your vision board.

On your board, you can add pictures of items you want - including that million-dollar check, if that's your thing. You can add pictures of new destinations, a building, or office that you may want. Whatever you want to add to your life, place it on the board. You can even cut out words from a magazine and add them to the vision board. There's no right or wrong way to create your vision.

Billionaire Sara Blakely, American business person and founder of Spanx, stated that visualization was one of her secrets. When selling fax machines door to door, Sara not only wrote down her goals, but she also visualized what she wanted for her future. She knew that she wanted to create a product for the masses and to be self-employed, and that's what she visualized every day.

Tip

Feel rather than *think* your way to the goal. Link your goal to a feeling instead of an object.

Your vision board will be the same for you. It's a way to teleport yourself into the future, and it allows you to feel what it's like to accomplish your dreams. Smelling the leather of your new chairs in your office or in your personal jet is great motivation. Hey… No dream is too big. In fact, the bigger, the better. You have to see it, feel it, and believe it. Create your vision board, and look at it daily. *YOU NEED TO SEE IT HAPPENING!*

ACTION:

GET **MOTIVATED**

1. List the *old habits* that need to be changed.

2. Increase your *self-discipline*.

3. Create your *vision board*.

"I AM A GO-GETTER
AND I WILL NOT STOP
AT ANYTHING TO
ACHIEVE MY GOALS"

I UNDERSTAND THAT
THE FIRST STEP TO
GETTING WHAT I WANT
IS HAVING THE COURAGE
TO GET RID OF
WHAT I DON'T"

3
MENTAL SHIFT

"IT IS NOT THE MOUNTAIN WE CONQUER,
*BUT **OURSELVES.**"*

—*Sir Edmund Hillary*

CURRENTLY, YOU PROBABLY fall victim to the contracting mindset. Our mind controls all that we do. It's where we make all our decisions - good or bad. It's where we decide that we want better for ourselves (like why you are reading this book). You wanted a change and decided to get it together.

CONTRACTING MINDSET

THOUGHTS	BEHAVIOR
- I should not eat that pizza.	- Chomp down a slice or two
- I need to do my work.	- Turns on TV
- I should research ways to start my own business.	- Surf the internet & social media

Notice that the thoughts in the model don't match the behaviors. If you have fallen into this mindset, you aren't compliant with succeeding at your goals. This is because your brain and thought patterns aren't in line with what your actions need to be to achieve success.

> Balance your thoughts with action. If you spend too much time thinking about a thing, you'll never get it done.
>
> – Bruce Lee

As I have discussed previously, you must rewire your brain. Inevitably, our brain operates from pleasure. The thought of coffee may bring you joy. The mix of tastes, the temperature, the flavor, and the aroma all trigger the part of brain that elicits happiness. You sip coffee not only to fill your stomach, but for the mere pleasure and satisfaction. With each sip, you target your brain's reward system, which is often known as euphoria.

Fact

Euphoric effect teaches you
to continuously repeat a
certain behavior.

The task that is left up to you is getting your goals on track with your brain's pleasure principle. Instead of thinking, *I should research ways to start my own business,* put it in the terms of feelings. For example, you may think, *It's going to be a great day to set my own schedule.* Maybe you are trying to lose weight. So instead of thinking, *I need to work out,* think, *I'm going to feel great when I'm thinner and can fit into smaller clothes.* Think about ways that would be beneficial for you if you achieve your goals. Getting rid of your debt may create a feeling of freedom and security. Finding love can create a connection with a partner for life. No matter what you choose to do, be sure to transfer it to a feeling that allows your brain to reach the euphoric state upon completion of that goal.

CONNECT YOUR
feelings

1. Rewrite goals to include a feeling instead of an object to *increase* your **success** of *reaching* your **goal**.

"I'M A DREAMER,
A DOER, A THINKER.
I SEE POSSIBILITY
EVERYWHERE"

4

BELIEVE IT
TO ACHIEVE IT

*"YOUR MIND WILL ALWAYS BELIEVE
EVERYTHING YOU TELL IT"*
—Author unknown

I'M SURE THAT it comes as no surprise when I tell you that only 8% of individuals achieve their New Year's Resolutions. Why do you think this number is so low? Here's my logic… Individuals are not serious about reaching their goals and if they are, their beating themselves with negative self-talk.

*Doubt kills more dreams than
failure ever will.*

Several times, I have thought to myself that what I really wanted out of life only happens to the rich and the lucky ones. Though I dreamed of a different life, I had myself believing that it wasn't possible. I convinced myself that I would *always* work a 9-5 for some company. I would *always* have to plan my one-week allotted vacation a year, in advance. I would *always* have to save years in advance just to afford the local trip. Oh, and let's not forget the things I would say to myself, such as: "I can't do this,"

- *"It's too hard,"*
- *"I don't have enough money to do it,"* or
- *"I don't have the right connections."*

That was me, everyday. I was unknowingly preventing myself from succeeding. Author Jack Canfield once stated, "**It's not what you don't know that holds you back. It's what you do know that isn't true.**" What we believe *is* our reality, even if it's far from the truth. Telling yourself that you weren't born with a talent or you weren't born into wealth are reasons why you can't succeed. These statements are a self-defeating, and they should be eliminated from your thoughts.

Carol Dweck, Stanford University psychologist and author, discussed two thought patterns of individuals. According to Dweck, one set of individuals believes that intelligence is innate and can't be formed. The second set of individuals believes that you can learn from your environment. She labeled the two-mindsets - the fixed mindset and growth mindset. The fixed mindset individual sees intelligence as unchangeable. Fixed individuals' development is hindered from learning and performing because of this one single thought. On the contrary, growth mindset individuals are those that believe they can learn anything, and they view failure as a learning experience. They use others' success as inspiration and motivation. The explanation of the different mindsets is beneficial, because it identifies how we can get stuck in one way of thinking. It also gives possible explanation of why we aren't successful with meeting our goals or getting to where we want to be in life.

Use this theory to evaluate yourself. Are you an individual that feels if you're born with it, you have it, and if you're not, you don't? If you answered yes to this, then seeking additional information to assist with shifting your mindset will be ideal for your success. Please note that this is not saying you need to believe in the fixed mindset or the growth mindset, but it is a suggestion to help transition your mind into a new thought pattern. What you were doing before wasn't working, so trying a different approach could result in a positive change for success.

Fact

The conversations people have in their heads either supports or undermines their progress toward their goals.

American actress, writer, producer, and director, Lena Dunham struggled with shifting her mindset. Lena did an interview with *People* magazine and revealed her negative self-talk and how it resulted in self-defeat. After graduating college, she would say things like, "No one is going to hire me, because I'm fat." She eventually changed her thought pattern and stopped believing the nonsense she was feeding herself. Since then, it has been reported that Dunham's net worth is a cool $12 million. Talk about a mindset shift! I'm sold! Where do I sign up?

Just like Lena, you have to change the way you think. Your mindset is the single *most* important piece in your success. Your mind controls all your internal and external happenings. Therefore, you get what you expect. If you expect to fail, then you will fail. If you expect to succeed, you will succeed. The beauty of life is that humans adapt when there are no other choices. Don't allow yourself to speak or think negatively; thus, success will be your only choice. Tell yourself, "I can and I will succeed." Be aware of the negative self-talk. Of course, change won't be instant. Nevertheless, if you put yourself on the right track, it will happen. Start with something small and work on replacing that negative thought with a positive thought every day.

Tip

Challenge your negative thoughts by asking yourself what are you getting out of thinking that way, if it's getting your *closer* to your goal, or making your *happier*.

Remember, you can't continue to do the same thing and expect to get different results. Evaluate your mind to become successful. You can do anything! Motivation will beat talent any day. Shining light on our negative thoughts is a great way to be aware of the ridiculousness we're telling ourselves. In order to achieve success, you have to believe it - even if you don't know how the requirements will be met. Like the law of attraction, we manifest things that happen to us. We will reap the vibes that we put into the atmosphere.

You have to believe wholeheartedly that you are going to be successful, and you must be willing to do whatever it takes to make it happen. Your brain is wired to do what you tell it to do. Think of it as a child. Feed it positively and nurture it to greatness. Here are several of my mantras that put me in a good mental space before I start my day. Feel free to use them for your daily morning rituals.

DAILY AFFIRMATIONS:

I AM **SMART**, **SAAVY**, AND **SUCCESSFUL**.

I **TAKE ACTION** ON MY GOALS NOW, SO I CAN GET TO WHERE I *want to be*.

I **HAVE** WHAT IT TAKES TO REACH MY *goals*.

I AM *starving* FOR **SUCCESS**.

I **ATTRACT** PEOPLE THAT ARE *successful* AND *like-minded*.

I AM **TALENTED** BEYOND MEASURE.

I **EMBRACE** SUCCESS.

I **REFUSE** TO BELIEVE *my own* **EXCUSES**.

I AM **COMMITTED** TO MY OWN SUCCESS.

I KNOW THAT *stopping* **IS NOT** AN OPTION.

IT IS **IMPOSSIBLE** FOR ME *to fail*.

"I WILL CHOOSE
MY THOUGHTS
AS I CHOOSE MY CLOTHES
FOR THE DAY."

5
SET GOALS

ONCE YOU HAVE created your list of goals, decide how you will execute your plan. Every great travel needs a plan to get there. When you travel to another city, state, or country, you create a plan to ensure that you arrive at your destination. Reference how you plan your travels, and mimic that to reach your goals. You decide on a place you want to go (written goal), you research the best way to get there (plan), you fly or drive to your destination (execution), and then you arrive to place of choice (success). Did you know that 60% of people that write their goals are more successful with completing them opposed to those that do not? Of course, I know you want to be successful with reaching these goals, so I'm going to tell you how to do it.

WRITE IT DOWN

If you have read this far, you already know what you want to achieve. Let's say you decided that the most important thing to you is being a part of the "new rich" lifestyle.

Fact

Using pen and paper, not laptops,
to take notes boosts memory and
the ability to retain and understand
concepts.

For the sake of clarity, this means that you want to pursue your own passion and make a profit from it. You are tired of that 9 to 5 life, and you are ready to transition to full entrepreneurship. That's a wonderful decision! Let's write that down. Now, when you write this down, you need to be as detailed as possible. Research has proven that the SMART goal is the best method to reach your goal. Let's discuss.

S – Specific: not vague; focusing on one
particular thing

SPECIFIC GOAL	NON-SPECIFIC GOAL
- I want to start a social media business.	- I want to start a marketing business.
- I want to weigh 170 pounds	- I want to lose weight
- I want to write a book about how to have a great marriage.	- I want to write a book.

Being specific helps you stay focused on what you are working to attain. It also keeps you from feeling confused and setting yourself up to fail. The statement should be so clear that anyone could read it and know exactly what you are working towards. I also like to think of it as my "request to the universe." I don't want the universe to be confused by what I'm asking, therefore the clearer the better.

M – Measurable: the ability to be measured

Measuring your goal is as exactly how it sounds. You will know your success when you reach the measurement set for that goal. For example, I want to weigh 170 pounds means I need to lose 20 pounds. You will know that you have reached that goal when 20 pounds have been eliminated. Another example is if you want to write a book and it needs to be 150 pages or 50,000 words. It's pretty straightforward that you'll achieve this goal when you've reached the total pages or words.

Some people get confused when they set a goal that may be more difficult to measure, such as to becoming a better wife. With a goal such as this, you have to first define what it means to be a better wife. For you, it may mean cooking more meals for your husband. Put a number to the amount of times you will cook in a week, and then you'll be able to measure your success with this goal. Pretty straightforward, right?!

Tip

Since *change* happens in small increments, figure out a tracking system to see your progression and keep you *motivated*.

A – Achievable: being realistic about the goal

At first, this one had me a bit confused. I couldn't understand what it meant to be realistic about my goal if I'm supposed to dream big. Anything is achievable if I put my mind to it. Wellllll.....after I did some research on the achievable aspect, I found that its true meaning is "being sensible on expected results." You may want to lose 25 pounds in a week, but unless you're going to have a procedure to assist with this, you won't do that within seven days. Making a promise to yourself for something that outlandish is setting yourself up for failure.

R – Relevant: something that matters
to you

We discussed this earlier in the book about setting a goal that matters to you. If it doesn't matter, you won't be motivated to see it through.

T – Time Bound: giving your goal a
deadline or due-by-date

This is the most important part of any and every goal you set. There is no way around completing this part. Though it seems irrelevant, it's the number one thing that will get you to success. You need an ending point to your goal. This ending date gives you more push to get it done before the time is up. It helps you stay focused, and you avoid setting vague a timeline such as, *"I'll have this done before the summer."*

TIME BOUND GOALS:

✳ I will start my social media marketing business by April 1, 2017.

✳ I will lose 10 pounds by August 30, 2017.

✳ My book for first-time married couples will be finished by May 31, 2017.

> *Everything you do now is for your future.*

USE A CONTRACT

After you have completed your goal list with your deadlines, put yourself under a contract. Treat this as a business interaction to bring more seriousness to your goals. Remember, we talked about this time being different, and it is. No more setting a goal and never following through. This time it is serious, so you should treat it as such. You are now your own client. If you tell your client that you are going to complete a task by a certain date, and you have agreed to this service through a legal bidding document, you are more likely to get it done. The consequences of not completing the task are unwanted. The same thing goes for the expectations you have for yourself. The consequences of being the same person and doing the same thing are unwanted. You are ready for a change, and that's why you are getting it together. Use this example to get you started:

I, _____, will work towards losing ten (10) pounds starting on September 1, 2017 and ending on December 30, 2017. I will engage in daily exercise for at least 30 minutes. My exercise choices will including walking, running, or an exercise video. After completing of my daily exercise, I will reward myself with 30 minutes of TV time.

Signed_____

Date_____

WRITE DOWN
YOUR *goals*

1. Set your goals using **S.M.A.R.T**. goals

2. Put yourself on a *contract*

"I DECIDE WHAT I WANT. I WRITE IT DOWN. I MAKE A PLAN AND I WORK ON IT….. EVERY. SINGLE. DAY."

6

BE IN THE KNOW

*"KNOWING YOURSELF IS THE BEGINNING OF ALL **WISDOM.**"*

—Aristotle

CONGRATULATIONS (insert crowd cheer)! If you have made it to this section of the book, you are clearly a woman about her business. You are truly focused on changing your behavior and being a better you. For that, you deserve recognition. Most people say they want to change but never follow through. However, you are clearly about to make some significant changes in your life that will help you get it together. I love giving credit where credit is due. Okay, so let's get back on track. Let's talk about how to break this goal down into easier steps to increase your chances of success.

KNOW YOURSELF

We have previously discussed that you didn't set certain goals because of what someone else said you *should* do. The same solution goes for how you achieve these goals. You may have read about an overnight success formula to become rich quick, but it's not true. You are going to have to work at it. I can't stress that enough that your success depends on you and only you. When you break these steps down for your success, you have to make the schedule work for yourself. There's no need to set a goal that requires you to work out seven days a week when you can barely get to the gym once a week. Girl, you know that's not going to work. Be honest with yourself. It is important to know your areas of weakness.

I have an issue with being distracted while completing a task; and, according to my grade school teachers, it was done very easily. I would always tell my mother that it was because someone made me laugh or someone was misbehaving in class that got me off track. The fact of the matter is that it's true. Years and years later, I still battle with the same issue. It took me sometime to accept it, but I had to be honest with myself. Then, I learned to work around this weakness. Being aware of your areas of weaknesses is more beneficial to your success than being oblivious to them. Let's use social media for example.

In today's society, almost everyone is browsing social media at some point throughout the day. When we're standing in line waiting to check-out, at dinner waiting for our food, or just simply bored, we scroll social media for hours to pass the time. Some people use it infrequently, while others cannot go thirty minutes without it. This maybe one of your weakness. If you are aware of your weakness to staying updated on all the hot topics or the number of likes you have on your most recent post, then cutting this out of your life completely could possibly be a bad idea.

> *Always ask yourself if what you're doing right now is helping you get to where you want to be.*

Telling yourself that you can't have something only tells your brain to focus on it even more. This will inevitably cause your brain to seek it more. Instead of quitting it "cold turkey," try setting a specific time each day to engage in this activity. Maybe you could allow yourself thirty minutes in the morning at 9 A.M., thirty minutes in the afternoon at 3 P.M., and thirty minutes as soon as you get home in the evenings at 7 P.M. With this, you are still fulfilling the need you have; however, instead of succumbing to your weakness all day, you are limiting the amount of time you spend catering to it. Thus, you are allowing yourself time to be productive on reaching your goal.

Fact

Additives increase the brain's production of dopamine (pleasure principle) and oxytocin (cuddle chemical) which is why you crave social media, soda, or certain foods.

The same applies to weight loss goals. It's not recommended that you stop consuming sweets if your body is accustomed to eating them daily. Experts advise cutting back little by little until your body is fully adjusted to the change. Use this same approach to reach of your goals. Be realistic about your weaknesses and address them. Your chances of success are far greater when you confront your issues rather than lying to yourself and denying them. I combat my distraction by working in a noise-free zone with my cell phone on silent. This helps me stay focused enough to complete my tasks.

Use the same methods with your strengths. Some people don't believe they're good at anything, but I beg to differ. I encourage you to know where your specialty lies and excel at it. Maybe you are great at time management. Use that strength to your advantage. Your time management skills can potentially help you create a great advance schedule, which goes well when you break down each goal.

KNOW YOUR OBLIGATIONS

When it comes to setting up your plans to getting it together, you must also beware of your obligations. These things are expected from you on a daily basis. Are you a mother who is obligated to check your child's homework or prepare their lunch for school tomorrow? Maybe you are a wife, and spending quality time with your husband is necessary in your relationship. Maybe maintaining your relationship with your mother is a high priority on your list - this is considered an obligation. We all have chosen obligations that have to be addressed.

<u>OPTION I</u>:
*Put obligations into your
get-it-together plan.*

Please note that working these responsibilities into a plan will require some major preparation on your part, but it can be done. You MUST stick with the plan you create so that you can be successful. What's that you say? That sounds like a superhero trick. Well, it isn't, but you can label yourself as Superwoman to make it more interesting. Follow these steps to setting your realistic schedule.

Write out your list of obligations (I told you, that note pad would come in handy). Think about everything you have to do outside of your daily hygiene routine and feeding yourself. Everything. What is expected of you?

Cooking? Washing clothes? An hour-long conversation with your mother or friends? These are obligations. Although you can't do everything, (sorry, I know the Superwoman thing made you think you would have super powers, but it didn't...my bad) you can at least make time for these things.

After writing your list, prioritize your obligations. What is most important or absolutely has to be done? Put a star beside the items that cannot be waivered. These should be at the top of your prioritized list. Next, create a schedule for the things listed. If your obligations are washing clothes, doing homework, and talking to your mother once a day, schedule them accordingly. When you create this schedule, stick to it. You will form a habit by continuously repeating your routine, and you're more likely to reach your goals. By having your goals as non-negotiable, you are saying YES to yourself being a priority and YES to getting your life together. A free printout is available at www.theamberdee.com.

OPTION II:
Delegate your obligations.

Delegating your obligations will free up some of your time. This is straight to the point. If scheduling a time to cook or clean is too tedious, then hire someone to maintain your home or pay for pre-packaged meals. Tons of companies offer their services for your convenience. Take advantage of them, and no, you should not feel bad about it. Using this method takes tasks off your plate and creates free time for you to work on your goal list.

Look at it as an investment in yourself. You are investing in reaching your goals and getting to the life you want.

Tip

You can hire a *virtual assistant* through Upwork or PeoplePerHour to complete small tasks online such as keeping up with your emails, data entry, and research for new restaurants, groups, or workshops.

· ACTION: ·

KNOW *yourself*

1. List your *weaknesses*.

2. List your *strengths*.

3. Create a plan that allows each to work to your *advantage*.

4. Choose **Option I** or **Option II** to address your *obligations*.

"IT IS OKAY FOR ME TO HAVE EVERYTHING I WANT"

7

BREAK. IT. DOWN.

"DON'T CALL IT A DREAM. CALL IT A PLAN."

NOW THAT YOU know your areas of limitation and strength, it's now time for the fun part. Let's CREATE YOUR SUCCESS MAP! This map will get you to your destination for success. It's what you have been waiting for, and now you're here. Your goal may be small or large. In either case, it needs to be broken down into smaller tasks. Kobe Bryant has been noted for saying that working towards a goal is like climbing a mountain. When you're looking at the mountain, you think there's no way you could possibly get to the top. Nevertheless, climbing one ledge at a time will result your inevitable arrival. Use this same strategy by breaking your goal down into smaller steps.

One day at a time.

When focusing on the bigger goal, it's easy to get discouraged and think that it's far too much to handle. You give up or tell yourself that you'll start another time, which never seems to happen. Instead of the traditional chucking of your goals, break your steps into small pieces. I mean super small. Like so small you won't truly notice that you're working towards your goal. For example, if your goal is to lose twenty pounds, instead of setting a plan to exercise six times a week, start with eating one healthy meal a day and track that on your calendar.

Fact

Breaking larger tasks into smaller ones will promote a sense of accomplishment and will bring one closer to the final goal.

By breaking these goals down into teeny-tiny tasks, you begin to build momentum towards your success. Each day, complete something that's going to assist you with reaching your goal. Remember, you can't reach a goal without action. A little step towards the right direction is better than no steps at all. After you have succeeded with reaching each individual checkpoint, reward yourself.

REWARD YOURSELF

You deserve it. Find something that you really enjoy doing and use it as a catalyst. No more watching TV because you feel like it. Make yourself earn it. This will build momentum towards your goals. You're going to need it to keep moving full speed ahead.

Tip

Select 2-3 things as *rewards* and do not allow yourself access to those things so that you'll be *more motivated* to earn it.

INVEST IN YOURSELF

I'm continuously looking for ways to increase what I already know. There's always more to learn. Knowledge is an investment, and you should spend it on yourself and your vision. This may include you purchasing numerous books, attending a workshop, or joining a webinar to learn more about the business you're seeking or goals you want to reach. Hiring someone that can lead you in the right direction is another good way of investing in yourself.

People seek financial advisors because they need guidance on managing their funds. People hire stylists because they need guidance on fashion. People hire nutritionists because they need help with identifying healthy food options. It's not a new process. It's the way of the world, and you're no different.

Seek someone in your field of interest as an advisor, coach, or mentor that can show you the way to become successful in that area. The quickest way to ensure that you won't grow is to think that you already have all the answers. NEWS FLASH…YOU DON'T! Open your mind to being flexible and open to new ideas. The more you know, the more you grow.

· ACTION: ·

INCREASE YOUR CHANCES
OF *success*

1. Identify **4** preferred items or activities you can use to *reward* yourself.

2. Identify ways to find a mentor or coach to **help** with your *goals*.

3. Break down your goals into *smaller* **steps**.

CREATE YOUR PLAN FOR SUCCESS

1. Name your **top** goal.
   Example: Become debt-free.

2. **One-year** plan
   Example: Erase all credit card debt by paying off all of my credit cards.

3. **Six-month** plan
   Example: Locate part-time job.
   Example: Negotiate decreased rates on credit cards.

4. **Three-month** plan
   Example: Sell items around the home.
   Example: Increase knowledge on negotiating credit card rates.

5. **One-month** plan
   Example: Meet with financial advisor.
   Example: Reduce spending by cutting down on cell phone bill, entertainment, and other bills.

6. **One-week** plan
   Example: Enter debt into spreadsheet.
   Example: Locate a financial advisor.

7. **Day-to-Day** plan
   Example: Locate all debt.

"I COMMIT TO THINKING ABOUT WHAT I WANT AND BELIEVING MY DREAM IS POSSIBLE."

8

STAY MOTIVATED

"THE ONLY THING A PERSON CAN EVER REALLY DO IS KEEP MOVING FORWARD."

—*Alyson Noel*

STAYING MOTIVATED CAN be challenging, but being held accountable is a great way to keep you going. I recommend joining an accountability group. These groups are everywhere for you to connect with like-minded individuals who support and push each other to reaching their goals. Now, I know what you're thinking. You're probably saying, "What if I don't want to tell anyone my goals." That's okay, too.

Tip

Set a weekly time and place for you to meet with your group to discuss *progression*.

When you're apart of these groups, you don't have to tell what you're working towards. You just need to give yourself a deadline and share it with the group. The members of the group will help keep you on track with your goal. If you don't know where to find an accountability group, you can join my group "Her Success" on Facebook. Visit my website at www. theamberdee.com and click the Facebook icon. You can also create your own group for accountability. You don't need a lot of people. It can be something as simple as you and your best friend, or it can be a group of friends from class or work. The key is that the group members must be positive, and they must be willing to help you reach your goal. *NO NEGATIVE NANCY ALLOWED!*

Fact

Achieving a goal you've set produces
dopamine, a neurotransmitter
responsible for feelings of pleasure.
Reciprocally, dopamine activates
neural circuitry that makes you eager
to pursue new challenges

Never stop striving for your goals. I know it may seem difficult at times, but you mustn't give up. Persistence is the key to success. 100% of successful people set a goal and reached it. They had desire, drive, and determination to achieve their goals, and so should you. You can't just be hungry for your goal. You have to be starving. The force of achieving your goal should be so strong that it pulls you out of the bed in the morning, and has you excited about what the day will bring. In the wise words of Winston Churchill, "Never, never, never give up." Now, I say to you….Girl, Get it Together!

INSPIRATION & MOTIVATION

Book Recommendations

* *Think and Grow Rich* - Napoleon Hill

* *#GirlBoss* - Sophia Amoruso

* *Year of Yes* - Shonda Rhimes

* *Like a Virgin* - Richard Branson

* *Power of Habit: Why We Do What We Do in Life and Business* –Charles Duhigg

* *Million Dollar Women* - Julia Pimsleur

* *Outlier - The Story of Success* - Malcolm Gladwell

"I WON'T THINK ABOUT WHAT CAN HAPPEN IN A MONTH. I WON'T THINK ABOUT WHAT CAN HAPPEN IN A YEAR. I WILL SIMPLY FOCUS ON THE NEXT 24 HOURS AND DO WHAT I CAN TO GET CLOSER TO WHERE I WANT TO BE."

Need more guidance?

This book is a great start to accomplishing your goals. However, if you need additional resources to reach your goals quickly or more assistance with creating a plan and sticking to it, go to www.theamberdee.com to choose a service to fit your need.

ABOUT THE AUTHOR

AMBER DEE is a masters-level Licensed Professional Counselor, coach, and consultant who encourages personal growth and professional development in women wanting to make the transformation to getting it together. Her real-talk approach to self-help and self-development has been used in her one-on-one and group settings to create a step-by-step personalized plan to help women get from where they are to where they want to be. To find out more about the author, visit www.theamberdee.com.

ENDNOTES

CHAPTER 1

1. C. Beuke (Oct 19, 2011). How Do High Achievers Really Think. https://www.psychologytoday.com/blog/youre-hired/201110/how-do-high-achievers-really-think

2. J. Zemple. (Nov 5, 2015). How This Entrepreneur Fought Her Depression and Built a $300 Million Business. http://www.inc.com/jessica-zemple/how-this-entrepreneur-fought-her-depression-and-built-a-300-million-business.html

CHAPTER 2

3. DuBrin, A. (1995). *Getting It Down The Transforming Power of Self-Discipline*. Lincoln, NE. Peterson's Guides

4. PrimeauTV. Tips for Success. http://www.dreamitalive.com/articles/Spanx-Founder-Sara-Blakely-On-Visualization-To-Achieving-Success

CHAPTER 4

5. D. Diamond. (Jan 1, 2013). Just 8% of People Achieve Their New's Resolutions. Here's How They Do It. http://www.forbes.com/sites/dandiamond/2013/01/01/just-8-of-people-achieve-their-new-years-resolutions-heres-how-they-did-it/#5a36bcf3304c

6. Dweck, C. (2007). *Mindset: The New Psychology of Success*. The Randm House New York. Publishing Group.

7. K. Hubbard (Sept 25, 2014). Lena Dunham Gets Candid About Her Anxiety and Body Issues in New Book. http://www.people.com/article/lena-dunham-book-not-that-kind-of-girl